Q&A

PAUL SCHLICKE

Foreword by
PETER ACKROYD

WATKINS PUBLISHING
LONDON

Dickens
Paul Schlicke

This edition first published in the United Kingdom and Ireland in 2011
by Watkins Publishing, an imprint of Duncan Baird Publishers Ltd
Sixth Floor, Castle House
75–76 Wells Street, London W1T 3QH

Conceived, created and designed by Duncan Baird Publishers

Managing Editors: Gill Paul and Peggy Vance
Co-ordinating Editor: James Hodgson
Editor: Susannah Marriott
Managing Designer: Clare Thorpe

British Library Cataloguing-in-Publication Data:
A CIP record for this book is available from the British Library

ISBN: 978-1-907486-96-8
10 9 8 7 6 5 4 3 2 1
Typeset in Dante MT and Baskerville BT
Printed in Shanghai by Imago

Publisher's note:
The interviews in this book are purely fictional, while having a solid
basis in biographical fact. They take place between a fictionalized
Charles Dickens and an imaginary interviewer.

CONTENTS

FOREWORD by Peter Ackroyd

Interviewing Dickens would be a challenging, if not unnerving, experience. You would have to be precisely on time. Dickens abhorred lateness of any kind, and would remonstrate with anyone who arrived even two or three minutes after the stated appointment. As soon as you had been ushered into his presence, he would jump up from his chair and shake you vigorously by the hand before uttering his familiar greeting, "How *do* you do? I am very glad to see you." There was about him an atmosphere of overwhelming energy. But he could also be tender – as tender as a woman, as one contemporary put it. And he would immediately put any interlocutor at ease.

Dickens had a brisk, emphatic manner of talking. He emphasized certain words in a slightly theatrical manner perhaps derived from his ubiquitous public readings, but he also had a slight "burr" or thickness in his voice that was sometimes mistaken for a lisp. Some people noticed a "metallic" quality in his delivery, perhaps connected with his prolonged life in the city. He never had a cockney accent, nor a rural one: he had the strange, flat, hybrid London voice.

In appearance, Dickens was more distinctive. He always wore resplendent colours, abhorring the familiar black of the middle-class male. In obedience to his injunction always to "Brighten it! Brighten it!" he might be wearing a scarlet waistcoat, bottle-green jacket and garishly checked trousers. In middle age he looked much older than he really was, having been wearied by a life to which he had contributed the work and energy of ten men. No writer ever laboured so hard or with such determination.

And what would you talk about in this conversation with Dickens? He ranged over a variety of topics and themes very quickly. If you uttered a word that appealed to him, he would snatch at it and repeat it. "Yes," he would say, "That's it!" He would abruptly change the subject. He spoke in a sharp and "jerky" manner, and gave the impression of a nervous, abrupt and excitable man. He would gesticulate freely – not at all in the English manner – and would rise from his chair to walk up and down the room.

Dickens had certain favourite phrases, among them "Oh lor no!" and "God bless my soul!" When he was listening to you, he would nod his head and often repeat "Surely" or "Certainly," and he had a habit of interrupting your remarks with the compliment, "Capital, capital!" He laughed freely and often; under the right circumstances, too, he was quick to turn the conversation in a comic direction. Everyone testified to the fact that he was altogether without grandeur or hauteur. You never felt that you were in the company of a "great author", but rather in the presence of an engaging and sympathetic man. He was a good listener. He was genial and responsive.

In his writing and in his career, Dickens became a giant symbol of 19th-century London and of Victorian society in general. In his brooding melancholy and in his broad humour, he represented the two great currents of English feeling; in his energy and optimism he embodied all the progress of the age; and in his fight for social reform he gave voice to all the progressive tendencies of his time.

And so, let your encounter with Charles Dickens now begin.

INTRODUCTION

Charles Dickens was the 19th-century equivalent of a pop star. The Inimitable, he called himself – and he was. Before the days of radio, cinema, television and the Internet, he attracted international adulation on an unprecedented scale. His first novel, *The Pickwick Papers*, written when he was only 24 years old, was a publishing sensation, going through multiple editions, abridgments, translations, adaptations, dramatizations and spin-offs throughout the century. Four years after this first hit, the serialized parts of the tale of Little Nell in *The Old Curiosity Shop* attracted sales of over 100,000 copies a week as the story reached its climax. In 1841, while still in his twenties, Dickens was granted the freedom of Edinburgh. The following year, huge crowds gathered to honour him when he toured the United States. Three thousand people attended a "Boz Ball" (the title celebrated his pseudonym) in New York City. "I can't tell you what they do here to welcome me," Dickens wrote home to his brother Frederick, "or how they cheer and shout on all occasions – in the streets – in the Theatres – within doors – and wherever I go."

With his long hair and outrageous waistcoats, Dickens played the role to the hilt. He cultivated a persona of genial intimacy with his readers, and built upon it by touring Britain, Ireland and America, giving readings from his works. When he died, there was public mourning, and his admirers felt that they had lost a personal friend. However, he concealed aspects of his life from his public – his long-term relationship with the actress Ellen Ternan, 27 years his junior, was still a secret more than half a century after his death. And to this day, we don't know for sure what the nature of that relationship was. From a modern viewpoint, it's inconceivable that they were not lovers, but Dickens idealized virginal young women, and a new anguish of unrequited love enters his last novels. It is at least possible that the relationship was never consummated.

If not quite the stuff of rags-to-riches fairy tale, Dickens's life has a distinct air of romance, and the writer drew deeply on personal experience in conceiving his works of fiction, not least in the creation of young characters who lead exemplary lives in the face of suffering. Oliver Twist, Nicholas Nickleby, David Copperfield and Philip Pirrip start life, like the young Dickens, lonely and sensitive, and neglected or persecuted. Despite this, they gain respect and security – and sometimes happiness and love, too. Dickens himself charted a course from financial hardship to considerable wealth, from childhood neglect to public adulation, from dubious social origins to a private audience with Queen Victoria. As such, his life serves as a paradigm of the Victorian self-help ideal, which elevated hard work as the way to lift countless individuals – even society itself – from raw beginnings to graceful sophistication, comfort and enlightenment.

Charles Dickens's reputation went into decline among proponents of the realist novel in the late 19th century – and even further into decline with the rise of Modernism in the early 20th century. But his popularity with the general reader remained immense, and the greatest of Dickens's critics, G.K. Chesterton, celebrated his works at the very time when the author's critical fortunes were at their lowest. Dickens's influence on later novelists has been incalculable, and since the middle of the 20th century he has been widely considered to stand second only to Shakespeare among English authors.

CHARLES DICKENS (1812–1870)

His Life in Short

In the last decade of a full life, Charles Dickens wrote a collection of exceptionally fine sketches, published as *The Uncommercial Traveller* (1860–69). In one of these little-known pieces, he recounts a meeting with "a very queer small boy" who aspires to live in the grand house at Gad's Hill in the county of Kent, the site of Falstaff's comically aborted highway robbery in Shakespeare's *Henry IV* Part One. The boy says that his father has told him that if he "were to be very persevering and were to work hard", some day he might come to live in that house. "I was rather amazed to be told this by the very queer small boy," observes the narrator, "for that house happens to be MY house, and I have reason to believe that what he said was true." The anecdote encapsulates quintessential Dickensian characteristics: a Romantic fascination with childhood, the Victorian aspiration to succeed through personal effort, a delight in literary associations, and the ability to transform a mundane moment into a dramatically compelling and deeply revealing episode.

Born in Portsmouth, Hampshire, on 7 February 1812, as the Napoleonic wars were drawing to a climax, Charles Dickens spent the happiest of his childhood days in Chatham, Kent, where his father, John Dickens (1785–1851), was posted as an official in the Navy Pay Office. Dickens cherished memories of his childhood between the ages of five and ten, not least because it was wrenched from him when the family fell into financial distress. Pulled from school, the 12-year-old Charles was sent to work in a shoe-polish factory in London, pasting labels on jars of boot-blacking, humiliatingly exposed to public view in the factory window. To add to the ignominy, his father was imprisoned for debt. Even after John Dickens's release, Charles's mother Elizabeth (1789–1863) was keen for her son to continue working in the factory to help to support the family. "I never afterwards forgot, I never shall forget, I never can forget," Dickens wrote bitterly in an autobiographical fragment published posthumously by his friend John Forster (1812–76), "that my mother was warm for my being sent back." This formative year remained a secret, closely guarded from everyone save Dickens's wife and closest friend until after his death. The experience left Dickens fiercely determined to succeed through his own efforts and to achieve financial security. And the profound sense of humiliation generated by his childhood ordeal left him feeling vulnerable and unsure of his social respectability despite his later fame and fortune.

When he was 19, Dickens fell passionately in love with Maria Beadnell (1811–86), the daughter of a city banker. Her parents considered his social and financial prospects unsuitable, and for four years she, coy and capricious, alternately encouraged his hopes and drove him to jealousy and despair. Two years after finally renouncing all hope of winning Maria, he became engaged to Catherine Hogarth (1816–79), the daughter of his editor on the *Evening Chronicle*. The relationship was tender and playful, but never ardent; nevertheless, they married in April 1836 on the strength of his contract for *Pickwick*. She bore him ten children, but in the 1850s the relationship came under strain. In 1857, Dickens met a young actress, Ellen Ternan (1839–1914), and he separated from Catherine in the following year. Ellen became his close companion, and perhaps his mistress, for the remainder of his life.

It was during these troubled years – the 1850s – that the house at Gad's Hill came up for sale. It was the type of idealized turn of fortune that Dickens accorded to the heroes and heroines of his fiction. By this time, he was author of a string of acclaimed novels, editor of a successful weekly magazine, a renowned public speaker, admired amateur actor, active charitable worker, respected family man and father of ten – and yet he felt that his life was falling apart. His marriage was breaking down, he was enamoured of a young actress the age of his daughters, he had broken with his publishers, severed intimate friendships and burned a lifetime's collection of letters and private papers. "Why is it," he wrote to Forster, "that ... a sense comes always crushing on me now, when I fall into low spirits, as of one happiness I have missed in life, and one friend and companion I have never made?" In this frame of mind, the 44-year-old Dickens bought Gad's Hill Place and moved out of London, where he had spent most of his adult life, returning to the scenes and dreams of his Kentish childhood.

Let us, too, return to the writer's origins. After his unhappy year in the blacking factory, the young Charles Dickens went back to school for two years. In his mid-teens, he took a job as a clerk in a law office, and after a couple of years began to work as a newspaper reporter. He quickly achieved a reputation for his parliamentary reporting, but his early employment gave him a lifelong contempt of lawyers and politicians. During these years, Dickens was an aspiring actor, going to the theatre "every night, with a very few exceptions," he later claimed, and being granted an audition at Covent Garden (though he was ill and had to cancel). To supplement his income, Dickens began writing sketches, which appeared between 1833 and 1836 in various newspapers and periodicals. Collected in two series in 1836 as *Sketches by Boz*, they attracted considerable notice, and he was invited by publishers Chapman and Hall to supply job-lots of writing to accompany a series of comic illustrations by the artist Robert Seymour (?1798–1836). Dickens promptly took charge of the project – "I thought of Mr Pickwick and wrote the first number," he claimed – and within months it was being serialized as *The Pickwick Papers* (1836–37). At the age of 24, Charles Dickens was a celebrity.

Dickens cheerfully signed contracts for further projects, but over-committed himself, and as his reputation rose "like a rocket" (in the words of an early reviewer), he became increasingly frustrated to see his publishers, rather than himself, reaping the profits. He met John Forster at this time, a lawyer and journalist who took charge as his unofficial agent, extricated the writer from the legal tangle and became a lifelong friend. While *Pickwick* was proceeding in monthly parts, Dickens became editor of a new monthly periodical, *Bentley's Miscellany*, in which his principal contribution was *Oliver Twist*. In a different key from *Pickwick*'s sprightly allegro, this story trenchantly attacked recent legislation regarding the relief of the poor. He wrote several plays and, long before finishing *Oliver Twist* (1837–39), commenced *Nicholas Nickleby* (1838–39) as a follow-on from *Pickwick*.

The link for Dickens between journalism and fiction-writing was established from the outset. All his novels were initially published serially, either in monthly or weekly parts; he wrote features, letters and reviews as well as novels; and, having resigned from *Bentley's Miscellany*, he founded his own weekly periodical, *Master Humphrey's Clock*. When this failed to attract readers, Dickens promptly turned it into a vehicle for two further works of fiction – *The Old Curiosity Shop* (1840–41) and *Barnaby Rudge* (1841). In 1846, Dickens served briefly as founding editor of the *Daily News*, and from 1850 finally achieved popular success as a journalist, editing first *Household Words* and then its successor *All the Year Round*, which continued to appear weekly for many years after Dickens's death, under his eldest son's editorship.

In 1842, having written five long novels in as many years, Dickens took his first break from writing, travelling to America on a rough midwinter crossing. Subjected to wild adulation, he soon grew disgusted by what he saw as brash American "smartness". Lack of respect for his privacy, the widespread habit of spitting tobacco and the sight of slavery rapidly disillusioned him: "This is not the Republic of my imagination," he wrote to his friend, the actor William Charles Macready (1793–1873). The author brought a storm of abuse upon himself by campaigning for international copyright – at that time an author had no legal claim on income generated by publication of works abroad. He further infuriated the American public with his travel memoir *American Notes*, which found faults as well as virtues in what he saw as a boastfully self-important young country, and yet again with heavily satirical American episodes in his next novel, *Martin Chuzzlewit* (1843–44).

Despite his fame and worldwide sales, Dickens's income had never exceeded his expenditure. In order to live more cheaply, he took his ever-increasing family to reside abroad, first in Genoa in Italy (1844–45), then in Lausanne in Switzerland, and finally in Paris (1846–47). He was to revisit continental Europe many times. The terms he negotiated with new publishers Bradbury and Evans in the mid-1840s at last brought appropriate monetary reward for his work and, despite the worry of supporting a large number of dependents, he was able to live in economic comfort for the rest of his life. With financial security came an increasing engagement in charitable work: Dickens collaborated with wealthy philanthropist Angela Burdett Coutts (1814–1906) in establishing schools for the poor, urban housing schemes and Urania Cottage, a refuge for homeless women. Politics, too, became an outlet for his prodigious energy. Although Dickens turned down more than one invitation to stand for

Parliament, during the public outcry over the Crimean war scandals of the 1850s he campaigned on behalf of the Administrative Reform Association, which aimed to shake the civil service out of its scandalous incompetence and red tape.

Between 1843 and 1848, Charles Dickens wrote five Christmas books. The first, *A Christmas Carol* (1843), is a miraculously poised fantasy of a miser's conversion – at once an engaging story, a social polemic and a skilfully crafted artistic composition. The Christmas books, along with special Christmas numbers of his periodicals, established a permanent association of Dickens's name with the festive season.

Dombey and Son (1846–48) is considered the first novel of Dickens's artistic maturity. With its depth, range, complexity and stylistic accomplishment, it forged new territory for the novel as a literary form. Over the next two decades, the author wrote seven further novels: *David Copperfield* (1849–50), *Bleak House* (1852–53), *Hard Times* (1854), *Little Dorrit* (1855–57), *A Tale of Two Cities* (1859), *Great Expectations* (1860–61) and *Our Mutual Friend* (1864–65). Any one of these would have been sufficient to secure his lasting reputation; taken as a whole, these books have profoundly influenced later developments in the novel.

Although success as a writer turned Dickens from his early ambition to make his name as an actor, the theatre remained a major interest. He was a member of the short-lived Shakespeare Club, a social association of writers, actors, painters and musicians, who met weekly for readings and discussion, and its successor, the Shakespeare Society, a subscription-publishing venture. He was close friend and adviser to several actors, notably William Charles Macready and Charles Fechter (1824–79); he wrote theatre reviews and was the prime mover behind several amateur productions, one of them given as a command performance for Queen Victoria.

This passion for the theatre found its most significant outlet in his one-man shows based on his writings. From early in his career, Dickens had given private readings. These became public readings for charity in the 1850s; and during the last twelve years of his life, professional readings for his own benefit became the author's primary activity. The most sensational of these renditions – the murder of Nancy from *Oliver Twist* – held audiences spellbound, and radically undermined Dickens's health.

In his final decade, he wrote only one novel, *Our Mutual Friend*. His marriage of 20 years had ended in acrimonious separation. His children, scattered around the globe in India, Canada and Australia, were largely a disappointment to him, and, especially after he was involved in a serious train crash in 1865, his health deteriorated. Never robust, despite the frenetic pace of his myriad activities, Dickens suffered a series of minor strokes and drove himself to the brink of collapse on his second tour of America in 1867–68. Although only in his fifties, he looked prematurely aged.

Dickens was at work on his fifteenth novel, *The Mystery of Edwin Drood*, when he died on 9 June 1870. It seems singularly fitting that the last words the author wrote – on the morning before he died, midway through this tantalizingly unfinished mystery story – describe a character who "falls to with an appetite". Such gusto epitomizes the life and work of Charles Dickens.

Q&A

NOW LET'S START TALKING …

Over the following pages, Charles Dickens engages in an imaginary conversation covering fifteen themes, responding freely to searching questions.

The questions are in italic type;
Dickens's answers are in roman type.

FOOD FOR THE MIND

Charles Dickens inherited a genre – the novel – that had been flourishing for more than a century before he was born, and he consciously followed in the footsteps of Sir Walter Scott, whose *Waverley* novels had brought new prestige to the form. A voracious reader since early childhood, Dickens states through the autobiographical voice of David Copperfield that reading "was my only and my constant comfort". He was also intimately familiar with the traditions of the miscellaneous essay, poetry and dramatic literature, to say nothing of popular forms of writing, such as newspapers, street ballads, tavern songs and the like. Each of these fed into his own writing, just as his legacy transformed the literature that followed him.

Hello? I'm sorry, I thought I was alone ...

And hello to you, my good sir, hello to you. How *do* you do? A stranger in these parts, if I'm not mistaken?

Yes. I've been tramping in the Kentish countryside all day. When it started to rain I was more than ready to find somewhere to stop to get warm. And then I came upon this comfortable-looking inn, The Leather Bottle is it?

My local hostelry! I live only a few miles away. And of course, it was the first stop for Mr Pickwick and his companions, when they set out on their famous adventures all these years ago ...

Shades of Jacob Marley! Mr Charles Dickens – I thought you had been dead these seven weeks ... But you taught us in The Christmas Carol *that spirits can do anything they like, so I'm as certain as I'm sitting here that it really is you, and no humbug. Can I offer you a pint of porter? Or a cup of coffee? Perhaps you'd like to join me by the fireside?*

That's it! Let me order a bowl of steaming punch, and we can settle in for the evening ...

[After a few minutes of small talk, the stranger starts to ask questions.] *I've always been a great admirer of your writing, Mr Dickens. May I ask how you came to the world of literature?*

Surely. My father left a small collection of books in a room upstairs, to which I had access and which nobody else in our house ever troubled. From that "blessed little room", as David Copperfield remarks (for his experience was my own), Tom Jones, the Vicar of Wakefield, Don Quixote, Gil Blas and Robinson Crusoe came out to keep me company. These books kept alive my fancy, and my hope of something beyond that place and time – they, and the *Arabian Nights* and the *Tales of the Genii* ... When I think of that room, the picture always rises in my mind of a summer evening, the boys at play in the churchyard, and I sitting on my bed, reading as if my life depended on it.

At an early age I also devoured the lurid tales in *The Terrific Register*, ghost stories and gothic fiction, and I was familiar with popular essays, poetry and song. My early reading was devoted largely to popular forms, but my schoolmaster, Mr Giles, taught me Greek and Latin to a standard sufficient to enable me to burlesque ancient myth, legend and history. Later, biography, travel, history and cultural writing –

as well as newspapers, journals and dreary blue books containing government reports – were staple food for my mind.

So you enjoy the classic novelists?

Defoe, Fielding, Smollett? Capital, capital! And the English essayists: Addison, Steele, Lamb and Hazlitt. Wordsworth's "We Are Seven" is my favourite poem – I respond with delight to the 18th-century sentimental tradition, and Byron and Moore are poets whose work I have read again and again. The names I bestowed upon my progeny might give you some indication of my predilections. I was going to name one son after Oliver Goldsmith, but changed my mind and called him Henry Fielding Dickens. Among my contemporaries, Edward Bulwer and Alfred Tennyson provided names for two more sons. I took my *nom de plume* "Boz" – a facetious pronunciation of Moses – in honour of Goldsmith's *Vicar of Wakefield*. But the author I have most admired, and whose example I took most to heart as a struggling young author, was Scott. Yes, I was intensely proud of the fact that my father-in-law, George Hogarth, was the most intimate friend and companion of Sir Walter Scott. Although only two among my novels – *Barnaby Rudge* and *A Tale of Two Cities* – emulate Scott's practice of historical fiction, his vividly realized characters, compelling plots and wonderful evocation of time and place showed me, more than any other author's work, what was possible for a writer of novels.

Then Scott's bankruptcy must have affected you.

Very much so. I took it to heart as a dire warning of the necessity of fighting for the full professional and financial rights of the author – both in securing appropriate contracts and in supporting proper legal arrangements for copyright. This campaign has led me into many disputes with my publishers, and it caused a furore in America when I spoke out in favour of international copyright …

So I've heard. You didn't start out as a novelist, however. What attracted you to essay and sketch writing?

The casual, intimate tone of the classic essayists appeals greatly. And the development of a friendly persona – Mr Spectator, Goldsmith's Citizen, Lamb's Elia – prompted me to develop "Boz", and later the public persona of "Charles Dickens". The essayists' evocation of contemporary London life and manners, their humour and sprightly satire struck responsive chords in my breast, and their development of clubs of amusing, eccentric gentlemen, such as Sir Roger de Coverley, offered a model first for the Pickwick Club, and later for Master Humphrey's friends who gather around his Clock.

Yes, periodical, miscellaneous publication is most congenial to me, and led me not only to accept Mr Bentley's offer to edit his magazine, *Bentley's Miscellany*, but later to found my own weekly journal, *Master Humphrey's Clock*. That quickly evolved into a vehicle for two novels, rather than the weekly magazine I had envisaged – but a decade later I achieved great success and satisfaction with *Household Words* and its successor *All the Year Round*. My "Preliminary Word" to *Household Words* encapsulates what I believe to be the essential merits of this sort of writing: "To show to all, that in all familiar things, even those which are repellent on the surface, there is Romance enough, if we will find it out ..."

Bravo! I know you are passionately devoted to acting and the theatre. Do you also read dramatic texts?

Certainly. I have studied Shakespeare closely, both on stage and the printed page, but I consider it essential to keep in mind that for all the beauties of his style and the profundity of his thought, his writing is intended for performance. That is true of all dramatic texts.

A CIRCLE OF STAGE FIRE

Dickens's life and work were saturated with theatricality. He was an inveterate theatre-goer, an aspiring playwright, and a gifted actor and performer of electrifying one-man shows based on his writings. The art critic John Ruskin (1819–1900) memorably summed up the theatrical element of Dickens's writing when he said that everything the author wrote was illuminated by "a circle of stage fire" – the gas footlights of the Victorian theatre. Dickens counted the foremost tragic actor of his generation, William Charles Macready, among his closest friends, and served as an adviser to his endeavour to revive serious drama. Macready, in turn, declared Dickens to be virtually the only contemporary amateur actor of merit.

You've been quoted as saying that writing is an essentially theatrical activity. Has the theatre played a role in your life?

I must have been eight or nine when my cousin first took me to the theatre in Rochester, where Richard the Third, struggling for life against Richmond, made my heart leap with terror by backing up against the stage-box in which I was seated. I came to learn many wondrous secrets in that sanctuary – one of them that the good King Duncan in *Macbeth* couldn't rest in his grave but was constantly coming out of it and calling himself somebody else! It was just one actor, you see, doubling up in bit parts after the king was murdered.

But even before that, my father used to perch me atop a table in the local inn to sing comic songs. We put on a toy theatre performance of *The Miller and His Men*, to which the police were called when the climactic explosion at the play's end proved particularly impressive! Later, I wrote plays for family theatricals, and when I was working as a newspaper reporter I went to the theatre almost every night for three years!

Did you ever think of becoming an actor?

An actor? Emphatically, yes. When I had just turned 20 I applied for an audition at Covent Garden Theatre

Royal. But being ill on the day, I had to cancel. And by the next season I was fully occupied as a parliamentary reporter … But I retained an active interest in achieving fame in the theatre and wrote half a dozen plays while my literary career was blossoming. Thereafter, I wrote theatre reviews for the *Examiner*, I was a member of the weekly Shakespeare Club, and an intimate back-stage adviser to my friend Macready during his tenure at Covent Garden, when he was attempting to restore English drama to its full glory. His restoration of *King Lear* (for the previous century and a half it had been staged in that wretched adaptation by Nahum Tate) inspired my thinking about tragedy and was very much in my mind when I wrote *The Old Curiosity Shop* and *Dombey and Son*. Yes, I have produced, directed and acted in a number of amateur productions, including a royal command performance for Her Highness Queen Victoria, and for the last twelve years I have devoted much of my energy to public readings from my works.

You mention Shakespeare – do you admire his work?

Shakespeare I hold in reverence. He was the great master who knew everything. His stories, his characters, his sentiments and his way with words are an unspeakable source of delight, and I am endlessly fascinated by his exploration of the relationship between imagination and reality. Like him – but tracking out his footsteps a few millions of leagues behind – I conceive of all the world as a stage, and it was a childhood dream come true when I was able to purchase my house on the site of Falstaff's aborted robbery in *Henry IV*. I had an inscription placed on the first-floor landing as a greeting. It reads, "This house, Gadshill Place, stands on the summit of Shakespeare's Gadshill, ever memorable for its association with Sir John Falstaff in his noble fancy."

Yes, Shakespeare's plays were among the first I witnessed in the theatre, and his were the very first books I consulted when I gained admission on my eighteenth birthday to the Reading Room of the British Museum. In 1833, I wrote a burlesque burletta, *O'Thello, or the Irish Moor of Venice*, which I put on with my family in a private performance. My sketch "Mrs Joseph Porter – Over the Way" (you must read it, in *Sketches by Boz*) reflects some of the hilarious vicissitudes of such a production. But in 1848, I produced a far more ambitious amateur production of *The Merry Wives of Windsor* – I took the role of Justice Shallow. What fun! We performed not only in London – at the Haymarket Theatre – but also in Manchester, Liverpool, Birmingham, Glasgow and Edinburgh.

Whenever I think of murder, *Macbeth* springs to mind; when I think of situations in which love and truth are tested, *King Lear* is my touchstone. One of my own favourites among the comic scenes in my novels is Mr Wopsle's performance as Hamlet in *Great Expectations*, barracked as he is from his first entrance until the end, when he dies by inches from the ankles upwards. As the acting manuals say, dying in a chair is perfectly unnatural – and anyone can die from the top down. What a coxcomb that Wopsle is!

Can you tell me more about your public readings?

Surely. From early in my career I read from my works to family groups and to friends. On one occasion, I dashed back to London from Italy especially to read my new Christmas book, *The Chimes*, to select groups. Later, I read *A Christmas Carol* to large audiences in aid of charity, and a few years after that, I began reading from my works for my own benefit. It brought in large sums of money far more quickly than writing. And I found the rapport that I could establish with an audience hugely exhilarating.

There were a variety of one-man or one-woman performances at the time – lectures, comic skits, recitals of dramatic speeches. My own favourite actor from childhood was Charles Mathews, whose distinctive act was a one-man show which he called a "monopolylogue". But the performances I gave were uniquely my own: I used no costumes to distinguish characters, only voice and gesture. I held a book, but I had practised so assiduously that I had the text by heart, and freely varied the words as the spirit of the moment took me. All the readings I adapted from works written early in my career, or from pieces I had written later, but in my early style. Some were comic – the trial from *Pickwick* was a favourite. Others were dramatic – the storm scene from *David Copperfield* was singularly popular. But the most effective of them all, which drove me to prostration but held audiences spellbound, was the murder of Nancy, from *Oliver Twist*. "Two Macbeths!" was how my friend Macready described its dramatic impact!

AN INKY QUILL PEN AND TWO DUELLING TOADS

Dickens's habits of composition changed as his career progressed. Three of his first novels – *Pickwick*, *Oliver Twist* and *The Old Curiosity Shop* – developed into extended narratives almost by chance, but later he planned novels scrupulously and wrote far more slowly. Plans and proofs for most of Dickens's novels survive, showing the care with which he conceived the broad outline of his story before beginning to write, revising as he composed. He never made major changes to a story after publication, but he did edit detail and punctuation in later editions, and at the end of his career started adding running descriptive headlines to each of his books when they appeared in a new edition.

I believe your first published writing was newspaper reports, and that all your novels have appeared in the first instance in weekly or monthly serial parts. Is your writing in effect improvisatory journalism?

That's it! When I was working as a parliamentary reporter for the *Morning Chronicle*, I began writing stories and sketches in my spare time, and these were published in various newspapers and periodicals before John Macrone invited me to collect them as *Sketches by Boz*. And so that early work, yes, was journalistic in origin. I based it on my close observations of London life as a reporter and also on the work of my favourite sketch writers: Addison, Steele, Goldsmith, Mackenzie, Washington Irving …

Pickwick, my first extended work, was conceived from the outset as writing to accompany a series of engravings of cockney sporting life. I was working within a well-known literary tradition of comic adventures. My friends warned me that a monthly serial was a low form of publication that would do my reputation no good – a prediction which the overwhelming success of *Pickwick* proved to be utterly erroneous! Although writing a specified amount to a deadline each month was hard work, I found it congenial to my temperament, and the popularity of *Pickwick* encouraged me to continue producing work in that manner.

Unlike other serial writers, I invariably sent my work in progress off to the printer and on to the public long before I got to the end of a story. *Oliver Twist* began life as my monthly contribution to *Bentley's Miscellany*, of which I was the first editor. After protracted negotiation, Mr Bentley agreed that the serial of Oliver Twist could serve as the novel I was contracted to write for him. It presented scenes of parish life, such as I had previously written as *Sketches by Boz*, connected in a continuous story of a sort I had been contemplating for years. My next novel, *Nicholas Nickleby*, was conceived as a successor to *Pickwick*, and before starting to write I travelled to Yorkshire as a reporter to investigate the notorious schools there. But the schoolmaster Squeers looms larger than life, don't you agree? *Nicholas Nickleby* is more than topical satire!

After *Nickleby*, I planned to write no more novels for a while and return entirely to journalism. I commenced the weekly miscellany *Master Humphrey's Clock*, but sales were disappointing, and the image of a child surrounded by grotesque objects fired my imagination so greatly that I simply *had* to develop Nell's situation into an extended tale – I transformed the magazine into *The Old Curiosity Shop*. When I was drawing that story to a conclusion, I drew up a checklist of characters to make certain I had them all covered by the end, and ever afterwards I drew up meticulous plans for my stories. Yes, although readers continue to favour serialized parts, the more time I spend writing, the more I become convinced that the public needs to read my works continuously – as a coherent whole – to appreciate their complexity and meaning.

You say that you draw up plans for your novels. Can you tell me a little more about your methods?

Surely. The tales that constituted my first four novels were improvisatory, but ever after I developed a method of planning that suited me down to the ground. Although I start publishing long before I finish writing a novel, the plot – the motive of the book – is perfected in my brain before I take up my pen. I go through agonies formulating the initial invention, and I simply must have a working title before I begin writing. Then I draw up plans for each instalment. I take a sheet of paper, turn it sideways, and draw a line down the middle. On the left side I make general notations and queries about the instalment; on the right I note down its essential events and characters. These notes serve to remind me both of what I have already written, and what is yet to come. Ingenious, no?

Marvellous! Presumably, if you must have a title before you can begin, your characters must have their distinctive names before they spring to life. How do you set about finding names?

Yes, the name has to be right. Nicholas Nickleby, on hearing that Newman Noggs has found the young lady he admires, instantly knows Noggs has identified the wrong one. Nicholas could not possibly have fallen in love with a Cecilia Bobster! Some characters have names I have encountered in life which seem appropriate for the character in hand. Thus, Moses Pickwick was the proprietor of a coaching business in Bath, and the editor of the first set of Shakespeare I consulted in the British Museum was Samuel Weller Singer. Bob Fagin was a boy who tried to befriend me in the blacking warehouse. Other names, like Swiveller and Creakle, point to the essence of a personage, and some simply sound right: Stiggins, Quilp, Traddles. I made lists of possible names for the hero of my autobiographical novel (having rejected the notion of calling him Charles), and I was delighted when Forster pointed out that David Copperfield has my own initials transposed. Between them, Darnay and Carton – in *A Tale of Two Cities* – also share my initials. I may have gone a bit far in naming one character Richard

Doubledick, but you can hear the echo of my name more subtly in any number of characters from Pickwick to Micawber. Some time in the 1850s, I began to keep a memorandum book in which I jotted down possible names and character traits.

That's ingenious. Do tell me more about how you find your book titles.

Yes, some of my titles follow in the tradition of "Life and Adventures", but I try out many names before deciding. *Bleak House* and *Hard Times* took much thought. I like the title of *The Mystery of Edwin Drood* because it leaves things enigmatic. Some of my titles are long and jokey: *The Life and Adventures of Martin Chuzzlewit, His Relatives, Friends, and Enemies. All His Wills and His Ways: With an Historical Record of What He Did, and What He Didn't*. Others are more simple: *Oliver Twist*, *The Old Curiosity Shop*, *Our Mutual Friend*. The book I had the hardest time naming was *Little Dorrit*. I had written several chapters with great pains under the working title *Nobody's Fault* and was on the point of giving up when I realized the book simply had to be named for its heroine.

And what about the actual process of composition?

Throughout my career I have always been methodical, devoting four hours each morning to composition, and rarely deviating from that schedule. I write with a quill pen, and I have a collection of familiar objects – including bronze figures of two toads duelling – carefully positioned on my desk. I begin by pacing the room, thinking about what I shall write next, then I dart to a mirror which I have situated beside my desk, and stare at myself grimacing and gesticulating, enacting the words and actions of my characters. Only then am I ready to set pen to paper. In short (as Mr Micawber would say), for me, composition requires my impersonation of the characters, which is why they always appear to declaim their speeches. This also explains why I find so little difference between writing a novel and giving a reading. Performance is essentially the same as composition, but carried out in public rather than in my study. I require a quiet, well-ventilated room in which to work, but I also depend upon stimulation when I am outside my study. When I was in Lausanne writing *Dombey*, I found the absence of bustle and plentiful variety to be found when pacing city streets a crippling impediment. Oh lor no, I can't begin to express how much I missed these!

THE COMIC GROTESQUE

Charles Dickens's writing was highly visual and strongly influenced by the grotesque tradition of the artists William Hogarth (1697–1764) and George Cruikshank (1792–1878). Much of Dickens's fiction was accompanied by illustrations on its original publication, and the author had decided views about what he did and did not like. He numbered several artists among his close friends – Daniel Maclise (1807–70), Clarkson Stanfield (1793–1867), Frank Stone (1800–1859), David Wilkie (1785–1841), Edwin Landseer (1802–73) and Augustus Egg (1816–63) among them – and his daughter Katey married the painter and writer Charles Collins (1828–73).

I can't help being disconcerted, Mr Dickens, by the fact that I can see right through your ghostly presence ... I think we should have another bowl of punch! Waiter! ... Seeing you thus reminds me of the very visual quality of your writing. Do you have a favourite artist?

Certainly. William Hogarth, without doubt. His compassion for the downtrodden, his eye for telling detail, his ability to depict sordidness without stooping to vulgarity, and the strong moral basis of his art all appeal strongly to me – no doubt because they are qualities for which I strive in my own art! One of his series of engravings was on display in my sitting room at Doughty Street, and 48 of his engravings hang on the walls at Gad's Hill Place. The notion of Oliver Twist's career as "The Parish Boy's Progress" was inspired as much by Hogarth's series of engravings marking the exemplary stages of moral journeys through life, such as *The Rake's Progress* and *Industry and Idleness*, as it was by John Bunyan's classic allegory, *The Pilgrim's Progress*. I particularly admire Hogarth's ability to identify not just the consequences of vice and degradation, but their causes. Take his picture "Gin Lane", where the reeling houses demonstrate some of the *causes* of intoxication among those neglected in society quite as powerfully as any of its effects. I find Hogarth's work a bracing tonic in the combat against hypocrisy. And in Hogarth's time, the distillers were as grievously outraged by this print as are the colliery owners in our own time who object not to the deplorable conditions in the mines, but only to the pictures that illustrate them.

[The punch is brought to the table] *More punch, Mr Dickens? What's your opinion of Hogarth's followers?*

The works of his followers, Rowlandson and Gillray, seem, to me, decidedly inferior. In spite of the great humour displayed, many are rendered wearisome and unpleasant by a vast amount of personal ugliness. It serves no purpose but to produce a disagreeable result. On the other hand, I greatly admire the work of George Cruikshank and of Hablot Browne. The reason that the illustrations by Cruikshank and Browne capture the flavour of my writing so splendidly is that both they and I draw inspiration from the graphic tradition of Hogarth. Like Hogarth's engravings, my writing is grounded on realistic detail – particularly detail taken from low life – observed with sympathy and humour and with such meticulous accuracy that it takes on emblematic resonance.

Can you tell me more about your collaboration with these artists?

Illustration was integral to the conception of my first published volumes and has remained a prominent feature of most of my novels. Yes, when John Macrone approached me with the notion of gathering my earliest writings into a collection, we had in mind from the outset that they would be accompanied by Cruikshank's engravings, and the book's title, *Sketches by Boz*, points to the closely observed nature of my writing.

My next work, *Pickwick*, began with an idea of a monthly series of comic engravings on cockney sporting life, which originated with the artist Robert Seymour, but truly it was my own project from the outset. I explained to Messrs Chapman and Hall that I was no sportsman, and then thought of the character of Mr Pickwick and devised adventures for him. So you see, Mrs Seymour's claim that her late husband deserved most of the credit for the success of *Pickwick* is sheer poppycock! And after Mr Seymour's death, Hablot Browne produced engravings under my direction, on subjects of my choosing. That was to be the pattern for all of my subsequent collaborations with "Phiz".

That's very interesting. And tell me, how did you and Browne work together from day to day? What was your procedure?

Before publication, I would give him a basic outline of the projected story, which enabled him to devise a cover illustration, and in ensuing months I would provide him with scenes or characters to illustrate for each number. He would execute the drawing – and might introduce details of his own – but the choice of subject and final approval were generally mine.

With the exception of Oliver Twist *and* Hard Times, *you collaborated with Browne on all your novels up to* A Tale of Two Cities. *But then you never worked with him again. Why?*

Our collaboration had run its course. His work became careless, and my own style had moved on. I began to work with other, younger artists as my writing became more dense and the fashion in graphic art shifted from grotesque caricature to more realism. There was Marcus Stone, the son of my late friend and neighbour Frank Stone, and Luke Fildes, who took over from my daughter Katey's husband Charles Collins when he had to withdraw on account of ill health. Over the years, several other artists provided illustrations for various of my writings, and others became close friends. Maclise painted a watercolour of our then four children for Catherine and me to take with us to America in 1842. Stanfield did the scene painting for some of my dramatic productions. And William Powell Frith executed portraits of Dolly Varden and Kate Nickleby for me. I have sat for my own portrait at various times, too – the best are by Samuel Lawrence, Ary Scheffer, Daniel Maclise and William Powell Frith, do you not think?

I've always admired the Maclise portrait. It seems to capture the vibrant energy that infuses your writing – and your life.

Did you know that when the engraving of that portrait was published as the frontispiece to *Nicholas Nickleby*, many readers thought that it was intended as a likeness of Nicholas, and not me. As if – ha, ha! – any fictional character could be as dashing as I was in those days!

LITERARY CHUMS, AND A SELECT GROUP OF LADIES

In the early 1830s, when Dickens was a struggling journalist and sketch writer, he met the novelist Harrison Ainsworth (1805–82), whose romantic novel about the highwayman Dick Turpin, *Rookwood*, had made him a celebrity. Ainsworth helped to persuade the publisher John Macrone (1809–37) to produce a collection of Dickens's journalism with illustrations by George Cruikshank, which became *Sketches by Boz*. They became firm friends, and Ainsworth later succeeded Dickens as editor of the monthly periodical *Bentley's Miscellany*. By then, Dickens had become acquainted with more or less every writer in London.

As editor of Household Words *and more recently* All the Year Round, *you seem to have been at the heart of our literary world. I hear you number Wilkie Collins, Elizabeth Gaskell and Charles Reade among your circle … but who were your first literary acquaintances?*

I met Harrison Ainsworth – at that time the most popular writer in London – while I was writing newspaper sketches. For a few years, he and Forster and I were constant companions. We had jolly times as the only members of the club we invented for ourselves, called the Cerberus Club after the wakeful three-headed dog of classical myth. Ainsworth hosted frequent parties at Kensal Lodge – where he lived after separating from his wife – and there I mingled with the convivial Thackeray, that dour Scots philosopher Thomas Carlyle and my artist friend George Cruikshank, who enjoyed a drink before he turned teetotal. I admire the pacy, gothic excitement of Ainsworth's historical romances, but the charge that he glamourized crime in *Jack Sheppard* did my reputation no good when that novel followed *Oliver Twist* in the monthly issues of *Bentley's Miscellany*. Bah! The press lumped us together as purveyors of "Newgate" fiction, when the only genuine similarities were that we both wrote about crime, criminals and prisons.

You mention John Forster who, it is said, plans to write your biography. Can you tell me more about that friendship?

Forster I met in 1836 and we immediately took to each other. We were inseparable, and for years – until Catherine and I parted – he, she and I celebrated birthdays together. Although we have had more than one flaming row, he is a loyal friend whose judgment, integrity and spirit I admire greatly. With his legal training, he was able to help extricate me from the tangle of contracts I unwisely entered into, and he became my most trusted adviser, routinely looking over my work in progress before it went to press, and helping me to correct proofs. Make what you will of his claim that it was he who first realized that, by my own conception, Little Nell must "necessarily" die! Like myself, Forster believes firmly in the dignity of literature, and again as I do, he cares passionately for the theatre. We acted together in amateur productions, and I wrote theatre reviews for the *Examiner* when he was editor of that paper. I honour him as a mainstay in the Guild of Literature and Art, through which he and I – and Bulwer, who brought his experience as a politician and novelist – tried to set up an endowment for indigent writers. And I don't believe any book was ever written half so conducive to the dignity and honour of literature as Forster's admirable *Life of Goldsmith*.

I modelled Tulkinghorn's rooms in *Bleak House* on Forster's chambers in Lincoln's Inn Fields. And pompous Mr Podsnap in *Our Mutual Friend* owes not a little to my dear friend, who has become increasingly conservative and respectable since he was appointed Commissioner on the Lunacy Commission and married that wealthy widow Mrs Colburn!

You say that you let Forster correct proof copy of your writing. Does this mean that you allowed him to change what you'd written?

Certainly! Oh yes, I trust his judgment implicitly. The best example of his participation occurred when, after dispatching the final number of *Dombey and Son* to the publisher, I remembered that I had forgotten Florence's dog, and so I fired off a note asking Forster to insert a word about Diogenes in the closing paragraphs. But with other writers, collaboration went much further. Wilkie Collins and I worked closely on a number of projects, in particular the play *The Frozen Deep* – I was deeply involved in the conception of the hero, my own role in the production – and the travelogue *The Lazy Tour of Two Idle Apprentices*, based on a tour Collins and I took to the Lake District and Doncaster. The Christmas numbers of *Household Words* and *All the Year Round* were written by several hands, either as rounds of stories by a fireside or within a framework I devised. And, of course, I routinely acted on my right as editor of a journal to intervene in contributions.

All the writers you've mentioned are men. Are you uninterested in writing by female authors?

I have no interest at all in the novels of Charlotte Brontë, nor of Jane Austen, oh lor no! But I do admire the stories of Mrs Gaskell very much. Indeed, her work seems to me a feminine version of my own writing. *Household Words* was the outlet for the majority of her short fiction and for *North and South*. But I must confess she exasperated me intensely over that work! She repeatedly ignored my editorial instructions, and I swear there were times when if I had been her husband, heaven how I would have beaten her!

I pride myself for recognizing at once that George Eliot was the pseudonym of a woman. I wrote to her when *Scenes of Clerical Life* appeared, urging her – unsuccessfully, alas – to contribute to *All the Year Round*. I had never seen such exquisite truth and delicacy, both of the humour and the pathos of those stories. In my letter I wrote that if they did not originate with a woman, then no man ever before had the art of making himself, mentally, so like a woman.

A PALTRY, WRETCHED, MISERABLE SUM

Dickens enjoyed cordial personal relationships with various publishers during his career, but there were also bitter quarrels over the respective rights of the author and those who produced the works. Conditioned by the experience of his father's financial troubles, warned by the example of Sir Walter Scott's bankruptcy, and faced with a large family to support, Dickens was categorical as to what he considered his legitimate income as a professional artist. Early in his career, his meteoric rise to fame rendered financial terms obsolete almost as fast as they were agreed, and he broke with one publisher after another. But in the end, he could command contracts that made him, in effect, his own publisher.

It appears that you've had complex relationships with all your publishers, starting with John Macrone.

Macrone published my early sketches and stories (most of which had previously appeared in newspapers and periodicals) as *Sketches by Boz*, in two series. I worked hard revising them, and they went through five editions within twelve months. Macrone and I were soon fast friends. He was set to be best man at my wedding until the ladies decided a bachelor should undertake that office. Macrone's financial gain from *Sketches by Boz* was very much greater than mine, but what rankled was his refusal to release me from an early agreement when Bentley offered me a fee two and a half times greater. Eventually, I sold Macrone the copyright of the *Sketches* for a fraction of their worth to stop him advertising the imminent appearance of *Gabriel Vardon*, the novel I had unwisely agreed to write for him (but never did). But then he prepared to re-issue the *Sketches* in monthly numbers identical in appearance to *Pickwick*. I need not tell you that this was calculated to injure me most seriously. I had a most decided objection to being thought to presume upon the success of *Pickwick*, and foist an old work upon the public in a new dress for the mere purpose of putting money in my pocket.

My *Pickwick* publishers, Chapman and Hall, came to the rescue, purchasing the copyright for twenty times the amount I had received only months before – and then found themselves obliged to issue the *Sketches* in parts after all, to recoup their expenditure. Despite taking in so tidy a sum, Macrone's business collapsed, and, although only 38 years old, he died shortly thereafter, leaving his widow and children destitute. On their behalf and in Macrone's memory, I organized publication of a collection by several hands, *The Pic Nic Papers*, which raised £450 for them. My recollection of the misery my family endured when my father was imprisoned for debt has made me particularly sensitive to financial hardship …

And is it true that you broke with your second publisher, Richard Bentley, not long afterwards?

Mr Bentley approached me in the summer of 1836, when my reputation was rapidly rising, and requested that I write a novel for him. After much discussion, we agreed that I would write two novels and edit his new monthly miscellany. But tensions arose immediately. Bentley was high-handed and interfered with my editorial prerogatives on the magazine – he meanly deducted payment when copy on the final page of an instalment fell a few lines short, and was stupid enough to advertise the imminent publication of *Barnaby Rudge* prematurely. Although, negotiating and re-negotiating, I had nine separate agreements in under four years, increasing my salary and granting me better terms, I nevertheless found myself earning only a paltry, wretched, miserable sum on journeyman terms, even as Bentley was accruing immense profits from my labours.

Before long, it was war to the knife with this Burlington Street brigand, and with an advance from Chapman and Hall I was able to burst the Bentleian bonds! I resigned the editorship of the *Miscellany*, purchased the copyright and remaining stock of *Oliver Twist*, and transferred the contract for *Barnaby Rudge* to Chapman and Hall. Bentley was one of the foremost publishers of the age, but I never worked with him again ... it was many years before we restored amicable relations.

I trust Messrs Chapman and Hall treated you better?

At first, Chapman and Hall dealt with me most generously, giving me a bonus of £500, a set of Shakespeare and a banquet to mark the first anniversary of *Pickwick*. And we worked cordially together on *Nickleby*, *The Old Curiosity Shop* and *Barnaby Rudge*. I remember calling them the best of booksellers past, present or to come. They advanced me the money I needed to pay for my first trip to America, and they published my *American Notes*.

But then, when sales of *Chuzzlewit* fell below expectations, Hall made the outrageous suggestion that my salary would have to be reduced, and I determined to break from them – a decision reinforced by paltry returns on *A Christmas Carol* soon after, despite huge sales. The rupture was never total, however. They dealt with my next Christmas book, *The Chimes*, and, sharing the copyright of my earlier works, continued to handle those titles. Up to the mid-1840s, despite the popularity of my works, to my intense frustration I never achieved an income sufficient to ensure financial security, and it was only after I had turned to Bradbury and Evans that my accounts with Chapman and Hall finally turned a profit for me. Chapman and Hall published the first collected edition of my novels after I finished writing *Dombey*, and when I decided years later to change publisher once more, I returned to Chapman and Hall. By then, William Hall was dead, and Edward Chapman's cousin Frederic ran the business. It was no longer the chummy personal arrangement of old. The firm had become a large commercial enterprise.

And Bradbury and Evans? Have you remained on good terms with them?

When I decided to leave Chapman and Hall – in 1843 – I proposed to their printers, Bradbury and Evans, that they expand their business into publishing, and we agreed terms that were more advantageous to me than any heretofore. *Dombey and Son*, *Bleak House*, *Hard Times*, *Little Dorrit* and three of my Christmas books appeared under their imprint, and they held a 25 per cent interest in *Household Words* (I held 50 per cent, the remaining quarter being divided equally between Forster and my sub-editor Wills). Matters proceeded amicably, with few hiccoughs, until 1858 when, wishing to quell injurious rumours at the time of my separation from my wife, I asked them to print a personal statement from me, which had appeared in *The Times* and *Household Words*. They refused! Such ingratitude! After all I had done for them, they proved false when my reputation was at stake, and I severed relations totally. I closed down *Household Words*, and they never printed another line by me. And I declined to attend my son Charley's wedding to Evans's daughter, God bless my soul!

My goodness! Tell me about the arrangements for publishing your works outside of Britain.

Well, since there is no international copyright agreement – you know how I feel about that issue – my dealings with publishers abroad have depended entirely on good will. Happily, my relationship with Baron Tauchnitz, who publishes my works in English in continental Europe, has been entirely amicable. Indeed, I sent my son Charley to live with him so that he might learn German. And in America my work is published by my dear friend James Fields, of Ticknor and Fields, in Boston. He and his wife Annie remain my closest American friends.

THE FAIR SEX

Dickens inherited his sense of humour and love of reading from his mother, but was permanently embittered when, after his father's release from debtors' prison, she attempted to send him back to menial labour in the blacking factory rather than to school. He failed to win the hand of Maria Beadnell, despite ardent pursuit over four years, and instead married Catherine Hogarth. In the first year of their marriage, Catherine's sister Mary was a frequent visitor, and her death – in Dickens's arms – at the age of 17 was a shocking blow. Another sister, Georgina, moved into their home as housekeeper and stayed with Dickens after he and Catherine separated. In 1857, Dickens met Ellen Ternan, the love of his later years.

Can I ask you about the women in your life, starting with your mother? You were a loving son, I'm sure?

Of course, of course. It was she who first taught me to read – master the rudiments of Latin, even – and I loved her sprightly sense of humour. She did make me very unhappy, however, when she wanted to keep me off school to work in the blacking factory. And she and my father drove me to distraction at times with their fecklessness. But I think you'll agree that the character inspired by my mother's exasperating traits as well as her endearing ones – the garrulous Mrs Nickleby – could only have been devised by someone who loved her dearly. It tickles my fancy that my dear mother never had the least suspicion!

Were other female characters in your books based on originals you knew?

Of course they were drawn from life! How could it be otherwise? I was very fond of Lucy Green (the name I gave her in my sketch "Dullborough Town"), to whom I was affianced, at the age of eight, in the haymaking time. There was true love! And when I was a young man I was utterly smitten with Maria Beadnell – I loved her to desperation. What I said about David Copperfield's infatuation with Miss

Larkins was based on my own case: "My passion takes away my appetite, and makes me wear my newest silk neck-kerchief continually. I have no relief but in putting on my best clothes, and having my boots cleaned over and over again ..."

A good deal of Maria's charm found its way into my portrait of David's child-wife Dora. But in connivance with her friend Marianne Leigh, Maria drove me to distraction, until finally I could stand no more, oh lor no, and stopped my futile pursuit. Years later, she reappeared, but although she warned me that she was toothless, fat, old and ugly, I was unprepared to find her changed so utterly. What had been winning coyness in a girl of 20 was (between you and me) grotesque in a matron of 35, and I recorded my disillusion – not unkindly, I hope! – in my portrait of the good-hearted Flora in *Little Dorrit*. As I wrote privately to the Duke of Devonshire, "we have all had our Floras (mine is living, and extremely fat)!"

You were married for many years and had many children. I know that the marriage ended unhappily, but could you bear to talk to me about your wife?

Catherine and I had many interests in common, and we shared much laughter during our early years together. She was a fine hostess, enthusiastically undertook roles in our amateur theatricals, and wrote a book of menus, *What Shall We Have For Dinner?*, based on our dining arrangements – it went through a number of editions. But as early as the time of our courtship, I had to remonstrate with Catherine, often and often, to get her to understand my duty to work hard. Later, she would never have managed our household but for the able assistance of her sister Georgina. Poor Kate suffered long bouts of illness and depression after each of our children was born.

Latterly, she became hopelessly fat and torpid, and our marriage became insupportable. Despite fame and fortune, I came to feel a yawning emptiness in my life. The separation might have been settled on friendly terms until, in collusion with her mother, Kate spread vile rumours, which were unforgivable. After that, I resolutely had no more contact with her. Save for brief responses on three occasions to letters from her, I never again communicated with her, even after the death of our son Walter.

I'm sorry … Your memories of Catherine's sister Mary are happier, I believe?

Oh yes! Mary was a lovely young woman – sweet-tempered, cheerful and helpful. I solemnly believe that so perfect a creature never breathed. She had not a fault. She was 14 when I first met her, and a mere 17 when she died – in my arms, thank God. In the first year of my marriage to Catherine, Mary was a frequent and most welcome visitor to our home. One terrible night, indelibly burned on my memory, she suddenly fell ill after a visit to the theatre, and expired next day. The doctors say she had a weak heart. Catherine and I were devastated. She suffered a miscarriage and I was unable to write, missing instalments of work in progress for the first and only time. I wrote the epitaph for her gravestone: "Young, beautiful and good, God in His mercy numbered her with His angels at the early age of seventeen." I wore her ring for the rest of my life. I dreamed of her every night for months, and it was with deep regret that it proved impossible for me to be buried at her side in Kensal Green Cemetery. I consciously reactivated my grief in order to write about the death of Little Nell. Later, when I was living in Italy, Mary appeared to me in a dream draped in blue like a Madonna, and told me that Roman Catholicism was the true religion for me. Now is that not very strange?

Perhaps since you idealized her so much, such a vision is not so strange. But (man to man), did you not have less spiritual feelings for other women, especially after your marriage ended? I've heard rumours …

Rumours! As a gentleman I have nothing whatever to say on that subject, beyond what I declared in the statement inserted in *Household Words* and *The Times*. And if I have to repeat it again, to you, I shall: "By some means, arising out of wickedness, or out of folly, or out of inconceivable wild chance, or out of all three, my domestic trouble was made the occasion of misrepresentations, most grossly false, most monstrous, and most cruel – involving not only me, but innocent persons dear to my heart … I most solemnly declare, then, that all the lately whispered rumours touching the trouble at which I have glanced, are abominably false."

I apologize unreservedly, Mr Dickens, for questioning this. Let's have more punch. Or perhaps a coffee?

DO TO OTHERS AS YOU WOULD HAVE THEM DO TO YOU

Dickens was a devout Christian, deeply imbued with a New Testament moral outlook, and impatient with doctrinal disputes and public professions of piety. Raised in a broad-church Anglican family, he was attracted for a time to Unitarianism, which regards Christ as a good man rather than the Saviour. He shared some of the anti-Semitic and anti-Catholic prejudices of his age, and vigorously satirized evangelical fervour, which he rejected as hypocrisy, as well as Calvinist gloom, which ran counter to his endorsement of sociability and innocent enjoyment.

You attack religious figures incessantly in your writings. Are you hostile to religion itself?

Oh lor no! What I thoroughly despise are public professions of piety, which generally mask hypocrisy. I am deeply suspicious of religious enthusioosy-oosy, which unctuous men like Stiggins in *Pickwick* and Chadband in *Bleak House* stir up in silly women. I have no truck with High Church flummery. Catholicism is no more than a system of social degradation. The Bulls of Rome (as I called them when writing to deplore Papal aggression) are an insolent, audacious, oppressive, intolerable race who perpetuate misery, oppression, darkness and ignorance …

As the Ghost of Christmas Present explains to Scrooge, there are some upon this Earth who do their deeds of passion, pride, ill-will, hatred, envy, bigotry and selfishness in Christ's name. Like me, the Christmas Spirit counsels that mankind should "charge their doings" not on Christ but on themselves.

Unless I'm mistaken, you don't extend Christian charity to people of Jewish faith. Your portrait of the villainous Fagin indicates that!

I have no quarrel with the Jewish religion, though when I was younger I was perfectly prepared to use the term "Jew" to describe a tight-fisted, miserly person – indeed, that was precisely what I called Mr Bentley when he was exploiting me as editor of his miscellany! I portrayed Fagin as a Jew because criminals of that sort often were Jewish – that is simply fact. But when Mrs Davis, whose husband bought the lease of Tavistock House from me when I moved to Devonshire Terrace, accused me of a "great wrong" in emphasizing Fagin's race, I removed most of the references to him as "the Jew" in later editions of *Oliver Twist*, and I went on to draw the character of Riah in *Our Mutual Friend*, an upright old man forced to present himself as a stereotypical Jewish moneylender.

You seem more concerned with life on Earth than with eternal rewards. How would you describe your moral outlook?

I say it's impossible to go far wrong if you humbly but heartily respect the truth and beauty of the Christian religion as it came from Christ Himself. Esther, the heroine of *Bleak House*, is the best example of a good Christian in all my works. Conceived out of wedlock, she responds to the accusation that it would have been better if she had never been born by committing herself to the selfless care of others.

Her guiding principle is to be as useful as she can be, and to render what services she can to those immediately about her, and try to let that circle of duty gradually and naturally expand itself.

I can't express my religious convictions better than in what I said to my youngest son, Plorn, on the eve of his emigration to Australia. I exhorted him to persevere in a thorough determination to do whatever he had to do as well as he could do it. I counselled him never to take a mean advantage of anyone, and never to be hard upon people in his power. "Try to do to others, as you would have them do to you," I said, "and do not be discouraged if they fail sometimes." I put a New Testament among his books to inspire him to goodness.

CAPTIVATING MOTION

Dickens travelled to the United States and Canada twice and sent his sons to live in Germany, India, Australia and Canada. His reading tours took him all over England, Scotland, Ireland and America, and he actively considered a reading tour in Australia. This *Wanderlust* is reflected in his work. In addition to two travel books, *American Notes for General Circulation* (1842) and *Pictures from Italy* (1846), there is much description of travel in Dickens's writing, from accounts of walks to trips endured on coach, omnibus and boat. With his family, Dickens lived in Genoa for a year in the 1840s, with extended stays in Lausanne and Paris. Later, he took frequent breaks in Boulogne, often accompanied by Ellen Ternan.

You seem to have travelled a good deal in the course of your career and you write about travel often. Did you enjoy travelling?

Yes, I found it exhilarating … for most of my life.

What was it that changed your attitude?

On the ninth of June 1865, I was riding on the express train from Folkestone which was involved in a frightful crash at Staplehurst. Eight carriages plunged into the river. My carriage caught on a damaged part of the bridge, and hung suspended and balanced in an apparently impossible manner. I got my brandy flask, took off my travelling hat for a basin, climbed down the brickwork, and filled my hat with water and worked hard afterwards among the dead and dying … I could not have imagined so appalling a scene. Then I remembered that I had the manuscript of an instalment of *Our Mutual Friend* with me, and clambered back into the carriage for it. Once I was home, I wrote to the station master to enquire about a gold watch chain which Ellen, who was travelling with me, lost in the confusion.

How distressing! You seem to recall the details most clearly.

To this hour I have sudden vague rushes of terror.

Perhaps we should turn to another form of travel. You and Catherine sailed to America on the steamship Britannia *– in midwinter, I believe. How was that trip?*

What the agitation of a steam-vessel is, on a bad winter's night in the wild Atlantic, it is impossible for the most vivid imagination to conceive. Every plank has its groan, every nail its shriek, and every drop of the great ocean its howling voice. All is grand, appalling and horrible.

Then, two years later, you moved to Italy for a year. How did you get there?

I took the entire family – plus courier, Catherine's maid, two servants and dog – to Genoa, and later Lausanne and Paris, in the hope of living less expensively abroad. We all rode a great, ponderous carriage through France, on a boat down the Rhône and to Genoa at last. It was a sleepy enough business through the countryside, but what confusion when we entered a town! The carriage would rattle and roll over horribly uneven pavement and instantly begin to crack and splutter, as if the very devil were in it, and by the time we finally reached the yard of the hotel, we were spent, exhausted.

How did the experience of living abroad suit you?

I loved the theatrical appearance of Italy, the bustle and the picturesque countryside, but the filth and fleas were ghastly, and I have nothing but contempt for the superstitious Roman religion. The most exciting adventure was climbing Mount Vesuvius by night, where we struggled to the brink of the crater, and witnessed the fire spouting out … We came back alight in half-a-dozen places, and burnt from head to foot. You never saw such devils as we looked with our charred faces and smouldering clothes! Lausanne, by contrast, was clean and calm and quiet, and the absence of activity deadened my imagination, making it almost impossible to write.

NOT THE REPUBLIC OF MY IMAGINATION

Dickens travelled to America twice, in 1842 and 1868. On the first occasion, he was greeted by enraptured crowds wherever he went. He arrived with an idealized notion of a Utopian society but, troubled by some aspects of American life, he was soon disillusioned. His hosts were angered by the author's demands for international copyright, regarding his arguments as a cover for self-seeking greed. Dickens recorded his impressions in a travel book, *American Notes*, and satirized American manners and morals in his next novel, *Martin Chuzzlewit*. By his second visit, Dickens's outlook had mellowed. In ill health and exhausted by public readings, he retracted his criticisms.

What were your first impressions of America? Did it meet your expectations?

There never was a king or emperor upon the Earth so cheered, and followed by crowds, and entertained in public at splendid balls and dinners, and waited on by public bodies and deputations of all kinds. I liked the people I met and the institutions I saw. At first I considered Americans to be as delicate, as considerate and as careful of giving offence as the best Englishman I ever saw. The country seemed positively Utopian. Oh lor me, I soon moderated my enthusiasm and came to a more measured judgment. But for the rest of my days I cherished personal friendships there – above all with my American publisher.

You changed your opinion of Americans, you say?

Yes, my outlook changed. It was precipitated by the Americans' response to my reasoned plea for international copyright. Friends warned me not to speak out, but I considered it my duty – in support of American authors as well as British ones – and the response was scurrilous abuse. I seriously believe that it is an essential part of the pleasure American readers derive from their perusal of a popular English book that the author gets nothing for it. It is so "dar-nation 'cute"...

Before long, I discovered that Americans have no respect for privacy, nor for an individual's right to independent judgment. There is no country on the face of the Earth where there is less freedom of opinion on any subject. Their press is a monster of depravity.

Goodness gracious! Anything else?

Oh yes! Their railway cars are heated to an infernal temperature and the windows clouded with endless streams of saliva from the universal disgusting habit of spitting tobacco juice. Above all, there is the accursed and detested blight of slavery. I got as far south as Richmond, Virginia, but the sight of slavery and the mere fact of living in a town where it exists were positive misery to me and I turned back ...

Upholders of slavery in America claim that it is properly maintained and controlled by "Public Opinion". Public opinion! Why, public opinion in the slave states has delivered the slaves to the mercies of their masters. Slavery is an abomination, and doom is as certain to fall upon its guilty head as the Day of Judgment ...

Did you find things much changed when you returned, after the Civil War and the freeing of the slaves?

I am happy to declare how astounded I was by the amazing changes, moral and physical, I saw on every side – in the amount of land inhabited, in the rise of vast new cities and the growth of older cities almost out of recognition, in the graces and amenities of life … And changes in the press, without whose advancement no advancement can take place anywhere. Nor am I, believe me, so arrogant as to suppose that in five and twenty years there have been no changes in me, and that I had nothing to learn and no extreme impressions to correct …

THE ATTRACTION OF REPULSION

In an era of profound social change, attitudes to crime and punishment underwent searching scrutiny. Population explosion, urbanization and new ideas about the individual and society contributed to the debate about crime, which was perceived to be increasing at an alarming rate in the early 19th century. The Metropolitan Police Act of 1829 introduced an organized system of law enforcement. Criminal law and administration also developed substantially. Dickens had first-hand knowledge of imprisonment from an early age, when his father was held in Marshalsea Debtors' Prison. As an adult, he routinely visited prisons and police courts, befriended detectives, and even considered becoming a magistrate.

You clearly have shown considerable interest in the law and its workings. I wonder if you could tell me something about that interest?

Certainly. After I left school and before I became a newspaper reporter, I worked as a clerk in legal offices. At that time I considered being called to the Bar – that is, to become a lawyer – a career I did not finally reject until two decades later. I even looked into the possibility of becoming a police magistrate.

On the other hand, I am acutely aware that the law is full of self-seeking toadies, hypocrites and rascals – I have done my best to ridicule such types again and again, from Dodson and Fogg in *Pickwick* to Tulkinghorn and Vholes in *Bleak House*. Besides legal wrangles with my publishers at various times, I sued one set of blackguards who plagiarized *A Christmas Carol* nearly word for word. But though I was wholly in the right and won my case in Chancery, the culprits fraudulently declared bankruptcy, with the result that they lost not a penny, whereas I was left with £700 in court costs! As you can imagine, this contributed greatly to the vigour of my attack on the delays, expense and complacency of the Court of Chancery in *Bleak House*. As my friend Mr Bumble in *Oliver Twist* declares, "The law is a ass."

But you got your own back – with interest – in your novels! You've often depicted the criminal mind. Have you come to any conclusions about the origins of criminal behaviour?

Criminal behaviour is, I am certain, most often the consequence of poverty, squalor and desperation. Wretched housing, hunger and hopelessness can turn otherwise decent human creatures to drink and crime. As I warned in *A Christmas Carol*, society must beware ignorance and want. But although much crime originates in such causes, it is also true, as I said of the murderer Sikes, that there are in the world some insensible and callous natures that become, at last, utterly and irredeemably bad.

And what should society do with such villains?

What should we do with them? You can surmise from my depiction of the condemned prisoner in "A Visit to Newgate" that I am appalled by the horrors of capital punishment. You may recall that I returned to the subject in my portrayal of Fagin's last night alive, before his execution. In 1840, along with 40,000 other souls, I witnessed the execution of the murderer Courvoisier, which I found deeply disturbing and utterly degrading to the mass of spectators. I did not see one token in all the immense crowd – at the windows, in the streets, on the house-tops – of any emotion suitable to the occasion. No sorrow, no terror, no abhorrence, no seriousness – nothing but ribaldry, debauchery, levity, drunkenness and vice. Later, I wrote several letters to the newspapers, urging that execution ought at least no longer be carried out as a public spectacle – a reform which did not become law for two more decades.

I recall that in Barnaby Rudge *you express outrage at capital punishment when you describe a young mother hanged for petty theft. Again I ask, what would you have done with such a criminal?*

Yes, this is what prisons are for. What I would *not* do is mollycoddle prisoners, treating them to food and lodging – to a standard far superior to the treatment meted out to paupers under the Poor Law.

And do you have equally decided views on crime prevention?

That's it! I satirized the incompetence of old-fashioned police in my portrayal of Blathers and Duff in *Oliver Twist*, but I have the utmost respect for the quiet efficiency of the officers recruited under the system introduced by Peel in 1829. Above all, I admire the able skills of the detective police. You may recall the detectives in my novels – the shadowy Nadgett in *Martin Chuzzlewit* and the shrewd Inspector Bucket in *Bleak House*. I number Inspector Field of Scotland Yard among my friends. He has taken me on his rounds more than once, and I drew on these expeditions in my pieces in *Household Words* describing the activities of the detective police.

WHY OLIVER ASKED FOR MORE

Famously, *Oliver Twist* contains a savagely satirical attack on the system of relief for the poor. In 1834, the New Poor Law inaugurated the first centrally administered social legislation in Britain. It was based on the doctrine of "less eligibility" – that is, providing less to paupers than the lowest-paid working man could earn, a move designed to discourage applications for relief. The policy was devised by followers of Jeremy Bentham (1748–1832), whose principle of Utilitarianism was seen by its opponents as cold and unfeeling. Dickens's criticism reveals his distrust of systems and institutions, as well as his fierce opposition to measures designed to restrict the activities of ordinary men and women or, in this case, to add to their misery.

You are known as a champion of the rights of the poor. Can you spell out your position for me?

Certainly. Although I would emphatically *not* support revolution to throw over the traditional structures of English society and I recognize that uneducated labourers lack the cultured refinement of their betters, it is my firm conviction that every man and woman in this country should have the right to decent food, shelter and common comfort. From close observation, I know that ordinary people are responsible and, given half a chance, prepared to be content with their lot. On their one day of rest, taverns are crowded, but there is no drunkenness or brawling. When such people seek relaxation, nothing but good humour and hilarity prevail.

When you showed Oliver Twist asking for "More", you created perhaps the most famous of your images. What made you so impassioned?

What Oliver needs is not just more gruel, but more food, more clothing, more shelter, more attention to his needs as a child, more kindness and more love. The law treats poor people worse than criminals, with no thought that a sick person, or a pregnant woman or a helpless child might not be able to look after themselves. The new system of poor relief that passed into law a couple of years before I began writing *Oliver Twist* was doctrinaire legislation founded on an utterly fallacious view of human nature. The "philosopher" Bentham and his followers – fool-osophers, if you ask me – think that human behaviour is motivated solely by self-interest. They have no place in their theories for the values that make men and women truly human: common bonds of love, generosity and selfless concern for one's fellow creatures.

I charted little Oliver's progress to show that someone raised according to these misguided principles would gravitate inexorably into a life of crime. What Oliver needs is not this sort of wisdom, oh lor no, but *more* of everything. Even poor doomed Nancy – a prostitute – shows more goodness in her loyalty to her murderer Sikes and her care for Oliver than Mr Bumble, Mrs Mann, Mrs Corney and the Board put together – those charged with the boy's care.

You're outspoken in your defence of the people's right to amusement, too.

That's it! When my friend Mr Sleary, the asthmatic circus proprietor in *Hard Times*, declares, "People muther be amuthed," he reflects my conviction that the English are, so far as I know, the hardest worked people on whom the sun shines – and therefore in need of respite, of more amusement, and particularly (as it strikes me) *something in motion*. The circus or the theatre, for example. Ordinary people know that, which is why they flock to the theatre at every opportunity.

I understand now why your novels are full of depictions of conviviality! I hear that you opposed George Cruikshank when he produced engravings and fairytales warning of the dangers of drink. Do you turn a blind eye to drunkenness?

On the contrary. Although drinking in moderation contributes significantly to the shared delights of human intercourse – as you and I appreciate even now, while we are talking – I am fully aware of the horrible consequences that drunkenness can produce. My early sketch "The Drunkard's Death" and my late depiction of "Mr Dolls", Jenny Wren's alcoholic father in *Our Mutual Friend*, are testimony to that. But I have no truck with teetotalism. Teetotal advocates are incapable of distinguishing between use and abuse. And, as I have drawn it in any number of scenes in my writings, drunkenness is quite as often the consequence as the cause of the condition in which the poor and wretched are found.

Drunkenness is a national horror, but its causes are many and do not begin in the gin shop. Commonest among its everyday, physical causes are foul smells, disgusting habitations, bad workshops, want of light, air and water, and the absence of all easy means of decency and health. Drunkenness begins in sorrow, or poverty, or ignorance. Yes, gin-drinking is a great vice in England, but poverty is a greater vice. If Temperance Societies could suggest an antidote against hunger and distress, gin-palaces would be numbered among the things that were.

Perhaps you and I have drunk enough for one evening. The rain has stopped. May we carry on our conversation out of doors, walking by starlight?

Capital, capital! On with your coat, and off we go!

GROWING UP TO BE A LEARNED MAN

A major part of Dickens's childhood trauma resulted from being withdrawn from school to work in Warren's Blacking Factory when his father's financial difficulties worsened. The boy Charles felt that his aspirations for success had been blighted. After John Dickens's release from debtors' prison, Charles returned to school, but the experience was not happy and by his mid-teens he had abandoned formal education, teaching himself shorthand to facilitate his work as a news reporter. Dickens took a keen interest in schooling thereafter, criticizing defective, incompetent and malevolent masters in his novels and working indefatigably to promote education for working-class children and adults.

You have devoted your life to writing as a professional vocation. Did you have any formal training? Or were you entirely self-taught?

My mother was my first teacher. When my father's affairs were going badly, she proposed to open a school and I delivered advertising circulars around the neighbourhood. Yet nobody ever came to the school, nor do I recollect that anybody ever proposed to come, or that the least preparation was made to receive anybody. When I left my mother's knee, I went first to a dame school – rather like the hopeless establishment run by Mr Wopsle's great-aunt in *Great Expectations* – and later to a fine school in Chatham, where the master, Mr Giles, was the first to refer to me as the "Inimitable". His school inspired me to hope that I might grow up to be a learned and distinguished man. When my father moved to London, I was taken out of school for about a year in order to work – at the age of 12! – to earn money for the family. Afterwards, I attended Wellington House Classical and Commercial Academy. The master, Mr Jones, was a violent sadist. You can get some inkling of my opinion of that school from my portrait of Mr Creakle at Salem House in *David Copperfield* and my account of "Our School" in *Household Words*. I was 15 when I left school and went to work.

For all that you say you value education, I understand that you didn't encourage your own children to stay on at school. Why was that?

As Tony Weller said of his son Sam in *Pickwick*, "I took a good deal o' pains with his eddication, sir; let him run in the streets when he was wery young, and shift for his self. It's the only way to make a boy sharp, sir." That's Mr Weller's way of saying that the education gained by experience is more valuable than book learning – although I certainly encouraged all my children to take a keen interest in reading. Miss Coutts, the philanthropic heiress with whom I worked on various charitable projects, paid to have my eldest educated at Eton, and then I sent him to Leipzig to learn German. My son Henry went up to Trinity Hall, Cambridge, and I have high hopes that he will have a notable legal career – now there'd be a fate for a son of mine! And my daughter Katey, who went on to become an accomplished artist, studied at Bedford College.

How do you think educational opportunities could best be advanced?

Anything that can lift wretched children out of woeful ignorance is a big step in rescuing them from a life of crime. Yet everywhere the churches and chapels prevent the development of schools by squabbling over doctrinal niceties wholly inapplicable to the state of ignorance that now prevails. I became interested in the Field Lane school in Holborn – the very type of a Ragged School, founded to help neglected and abandoned children. Such schools were necessarily imperfect, but provided a stopgap to an urgent social problem until Forster's Education Bill came before Parliament in February this year.

I devoted much energy to Ragged Schools, visiting them often, enlisting financial support from Miss Coutts, petitioning the government – unsuccessfully, of course – and writing letters and articles to rouse public interest. I even considered founding a school in collaboration with our foremost educational reformer, Sir James Kay-Shuttleworth. I do not hesitate to say – why should I, for I know it to be true! – that an annual sum of money granted to these schools and unhindered by red tape would relieve the prisons, diminish our taxes, clear loads of shame and guilt out of the streets, recruit for the army and navy, and waft to new countries fleets full of useful labour.

You're also interested in adult education, are you not?

Yes, as my young friend David Copperfield says, I never could have done what I have done without the habits of punctuality, order and diligence and without the determination to concentrate on one object at a time, no matter how quickly its successor should come upon its heels. Whatever I have devoted myself to, I have devoted myself to completely. Happily, there are organizations throughout the land dedicated to facilitating such self-help – the Mechanics' Institutes, which offer lectures, classes and libraries to promote learning of all sorts.

FAITH IN THE PEOPLE

From his experience as a reporter, covering elections, speeches and parliamentary debates, Dickens developed a hearty contempt for politics and politicians. The Circumlocution Office in *Little Dorrit*, containing "the whole science of government" – that is, "how not to do it" – epitomizes his belief that politicians were either knaves or fools. On the other hand, Dickens was viewed as an outspoken radical for championing the common man in the reform era, in opposition to the Tories, who feared that the erosion of traditional privilege would lead to anarchy and bloodshed. Dickens declined offers to stand for parliament, but took an active part in the public outcry over government mismanagement in the Crimean War.

Could I enquire about your outlook on politics?

Certainly. I stated my credo in a speech to the Birmingham and Midland Institute in 1869, when I announced that "My faith in the people governing, is, on the whole, infinitesimal; my faith in The People governed is, on the whole illimitable." The full title of my first book was *Sketches by Boz, Illustrative of Everyday Life, and Everyday People*. It may take a leap of imagination now to realize how contentious such a title was then: it assumes that an ordinary man or woman is as important and as worthy of interest as a king or a lord! Yes, this was at a time when reactionary Tories were fighting tooth and nail to hang on to vested privilege. At the Northamptonshire election in 1835 I witnessed a body of horsemen in the Tory interest charge a mob with bludgeons with a degree of brutal violence of which no description can give an adequate idea. This body was headed by a parson, who produced from his coat a pistol, and levelled it at a person in the crowd … Such a ruthless set of bloody-minded villains I never set eyes on in my life.

Did you consider running for office yourself?

I never *sought* selection, but I was approached on several occasions. I must admit I was tempted in 1841 by the Liberal agent for Reading, but at that time I could not afford the expense, particularly since the Conservatives were almost certain to win the seat. I was never again so tempted. In 1868 it was proposed to me, under very flattering circumstances indeed, to come in as the Third Member for Birmingham. I replied in what became my stereotyped phrase, that no consideration on Earth would induce me to become a candidate for the representation of any place in the House of Commons. That arena – its irrationality and dishonesty – is quite shocking.

I gather from this that you dislike all politicians, to a man.

Not quite. I must admit that I was fond of Talfourd – the circuit judge and playwright. He was an effective politician. In appreciation of his efforts to reform copyright law, I dedicated *Pickwick* to him.

But the politician with whom I have most engaged in things political is Lord Russell. I admire his stand on political and educational reform, and I vividly recall during my reporting days transcribing one of his election speeches in the midst of a lively fight carried on by all the vagabonds in that part of the county. When he was Prime Minister, I was not reticent about giving him a little bit of truth about current affairs. I dedicated *A Tale of Two Cities* to him.

A CAREFREE ESCAPE

Dickens was not robust as a child, and allowed, when describing an offer to write about sporting life, that he was "no great sportsman except in regard of all kinds of locomotion". He was an obsessive walker, traversing miles daily, especially in city streets and at night. At Gad's Hill, he engaged in bar leaping, bowling and quoits, and sponsored the local cricket club, who played on his fields. Dickens took a keen interest, too, in the theatre and circus. In his works he focuses on the enjoyment and fellow-feeling of spectators escaping the daily toil of mundane reality at such performances, and on their stimulus to imagination, or "fancy". But the amusement most intimately associated with his life and works is the celebration of Christmas.

In the Preface to Pickwick *you admit that you are not a sportsman, but you've certainly led an active life ...*

It's true that I have never been athletic and that I have no sympathy for the sporting set, but I have always delighted in cricket. Yes, I vividly recall the cricket field in the village where I grew up, usurped now, alas, by the railway. You will recall that there is a convivial cricket match in *Pickwick* between Dingley Dell and the All-Muggletonians, and that Little Nell finds relief from her travels when she comes upon cricket on the green. After I moved to Gad's Hill I promoted cricket matches in the grounds.

Although, as I made clear in *Nickleby*, I deplore the debauchery associated with prize-fighting, I did invite my friend Layard to accompany me to the Sayer versus Heenan championship bout in 1860, and I have published a number of articles about "The Fancy" (as Pierce Egan described pugilism). In 1866, I held a gala sports day which attracted some 2,000 souls to Gad's Hill. I particularly remember one contestant who came in second in the hurdles race, vigorously puffing on his pipe the entire way. "If it hadn't been for your pipe," I said to him at the winning-post, "you would have been first." "I beg your pardon, sir," he answered, "but if it hadn't been for my pipe, I should have been nowhere." What larks!

What about your own participation?

I have been an inveterate pedestrian all my life – not in competition I admit, but as a hugely enjoyable activity in company or alone. Yes, hardly a day goes by that I do not walk for miles. It is an opportunity for the close observation that is an essential ingredient in my writing – and when I lack city streets I keenly miss their stimulus to my fancy. Several of my characters undertake marathon hikes. My last special feat was turning out of bed at two, after a hard day, pedestrian and otherwise, and walking thirty miles into the country for breakfast – from Tavistock House in London to Gad's Hill Place in Kent! And when I was discouraged by lameness and ill health during my second visit to America, my readings manager, "The Man of Ross", organized a pedestrian race of twelve miles against my American publisher, "The Boston Bantam". Yours truly, "The Gad's Hill Gasper", acted as referee, and the event cheered me splendidly.

What larks, indeed! It's said that the circus is another of your favourite activities. What is it that attracts you?

I love the spectacle, the movement, the skill and the colour – and the mysterious beings in costumes of gods and sylphs. It is delightful, splendid and surprising.

I wrote about the circus in *Hard Times*, of course, and published a sketch on England's foremost circus, Astley's, in *Sketches by Boz*. I sent Kit and Barbara (in *The Old Curiosity Shop*) there with their families on their half-holiday, and Trooper George in *Bleak House* goes for relief from his troubles. One summer, when I was on holiday in Broadstairs, I got caught up in a whirl of dissipation when I found a female lion-tamer performing nearby. I wrote to my dear friend Beard that he had missed wild beasts at Ramsgate and a young lady in armour, who went into the dens while a rustic keeper who spoke through his nose exclaimed, "Beold the abazid power of woobud!" At the Cirque Franconi in Paris, I saw the clown from Astley's receive a rapturous reception. His name was Boswell and the whole *cirque* rang with cries for Boz Zwillll! Boz Zweellll! Yes, as you may gather, I enjoy the circus!

Finally, I must find out what lies behind the perception which has been widespread following A Christmas Carol, *that you single-handedly invented Christmas. Is there any truth in this?*

Oh lor no! Christmas celebrations had been around a good long while before I came upon the scene! They simply were not fashionable when I was young. But as my accounts in *Sketches by Boz* and *The Pickwick*

Papers attest, Christmas emphatically was honoured when I first began writing about it. When I followed on from the *Carol* with *The Chimes* and *The Cricket on the Hearth*, my public came to expect Christmas writing from me, whether stories *about* Christmas or stories *for* Christmas, and whether written solely by me or in collaboration with others in the special Christmas numbers of *Household Words* and *All the Year Round*.

I certainly celebrate Christmas heartily in my own home, with charades and magic and games – all the merrier because my eldest son Charley has the good fortune of celebrating his birthday on Twelfth Night. Mind, Christmas for me is not simply a time of jollity, but a time to take stock, to renew family ties, to face up to sorrows, fears and hardship. Yes, it is a time of storytelling, of memory and togetherness – a time for compassion and contentment. Like Scrooge's nephew, I have always thought of Christmas as a kind, forgiving, charitable, pleasant time. The only time in the long calendar of the year when men and women open their shut-up hearts freely, and think of people below them as if they really were fellow-passengers to the grave. And therefore I believe that Christmas has done me good; and I say, "God bless it!"

[And with these words the ghost of Charles Dickens fades into the night, and the interview is at an end ...]

FURTHER RESEARCH

THE CHARLES DICKENS MUSEUM

This book was written in aid of the Charles Dickens Museum, 48 Doughty Street, London (www.dickensmuseum.com). Built in 1801, this is the only London residence of Dickens still standing. He rented the Georgian terraced house from April 1837 to December 1839, moving in with his wife and infant son and writing *The Pickwick Papers*, *Oliver Twist* and *Nicholas Nickleby* there. Dickens's daughters Katey and Mamie were born in Doughty Street and his sister-in-law Mary Hogarth died in Dickens's arms there. Purchased by the Dickens Fellowship in 1923, the house is open to the public and provides facilities for researchers.

BIBLIOGRAPHY

WORKS BY DICKENS

Novels, Christmas books, travel books, and collections authorized by Dickens:

Sketches by Boz, first and second series (1836)
The Pickwick Papers (1836–37)
Oliver Twist (1837–39)
Nicholas Nickleby (1838–39)
The Old Curiosity Shop (1840–41)
Barnaby Rudge (1841)
American Notes (1842)
Martin Chuzzlewit (1843–44)
A Christmas Carol (1843)
The Chimes (1844)
The Cricket on the Hearth (1845)
Pictures from Italy (1846)
Dombey and Son (1846–48)
The Battle of Life (1846)
The Haunted Man (1848)
David Copperfield (1849–50)
Bleak House (1852–53)
Hard Times (1854)
Little Dorrit (1855–57)
Reprinted Pieces (1858)
A Tale of Two Cities (1859)
Christmas Stories (1859)
The Uncommercial Traveller (1860)
Great Expectations (1861)
Our Mutual Friend (1864–65)
The Mystery of Edwin Drood (1870)

OTHER WRITINGS BY DICKENS

The Letters of Charles Dickens The British Academy / Pilgrim edition eds. Graham Storey et al. (Oxford: Clarendon, 1965–2002; 12 vols)
The Speeches of Charles Dickens ed. K.J. Fielding (Oxford: Clarendon, 1960)

A generous sampling of Dickens's works as a journalist are collected in Michael Slater (ed.) *Dickens' Journalism* (London: Dent, 1994–2000; 4 vols).

BOOKS ABOUT DICKENS

Peter Ackroyd, *Dickens* (London: Sinclair-Stevenson, 1990)

Phillip Collins, *Dickens and Crime* (London: Macmillan, 1965, second edition)
Phillip Collins, *Dickens and Education* (London: Macmillan, 1963)
Phillip Collins (ed.), *Dickens: Interviews and Recollections* (London: Macmillan, 1981)
Mamie Dickens, *My Father As I Recall Him* (London: Roxburghe Press, 1897)
John Forster, *The Life of Charles Dickens* ed. J.W.T. Ley (London: Cecil Palmer, 1928)
Robin Gilmour, *The Idea of the Gentleman in the Victorian Novel* (London: Allen and Unwin, 1981)
Edgar Johnson, *Charles Dickens: His Tragedy and Triumph*. (Boston: Little, Brown, 1952)
Paul Schlicke (ed.), *Oxford Reader's Companion to Dickens* (Oxford: Oxford University Press, 1999)

NOTES

Quotations from *The Letters of Charles Dickens* (eds. Graham Storey et al.) by permission of Oxford University Press.

p.9 **"I can't tell you ... wherever I go"** Pilgrim, *Letters*, 3.37
p.10–11 **his life serves as a paradigm ... sophistication, comfort and enlightenment** This argument is indebted to Gilmour, pp.120–23
p.13 **"I never afterwards forgot ... being sent back"** Forster, 1.2.35
p.15 **"Why is it ... never made?"** Forster, 8.2.639
p.15 **"every night, with a very few exceptions,"** *Letters*, 4.245
p.17 **"This is not the Republic of my imagination"** *Letters*, 3.156
p.29 **the most intimate friend and companion of Sir Walter Scott** *Letters*, 1.144
p.36 **an unspeakable source of delight** *Letters*, 3.165
p.37 **"This house ... in his noble fancy"** Forster, 8.3.652
p.39 **"Two Macbeths!"** *Letters*, 12.291
p.52 **grievously outraged ... illustrate them** *Letters* 3.284
p.59 **"necessarily" die** Forster, 2.7.151
p.59 **I don't believe ... honour of literature** *Letters*, 5.289
p.60 **I fired off a note ... closing paragraphs** *Letters*, 5.264
p.61 **if I had been her husband, heaven how I would have beaten her!** based on *Letters*, 7.700
p.61 **exquisite truth and delicacy ... so like a woman** *Letters*, 8.506
p.64 **I need not tell you ... money in my pocket** *Letters*, 1.269–70
p.66 **a paltry, wretched, miserable sum ... immense profits** *Letters*, 1.493
p.66 **war to the knife ... burst the Bentleian bonds** *Letters*, 1.504, 619

p.66–7 **the best of booksellers past, present or to come** *Letters* 1.601–2
p.75 **was toothless, fat, old and ugly** *Oxford Companion*, 34
p.75 **"we have all had our Floras (mine is living, and extremely fat)"** *Letters*, 8.149
p.75–6 **I solemnly believe ... not a fault** *Letters*, 1.259
p.76 **"Young, beautiful and good ... age of seventeen"** *Oxford Companion*, 274
p.82 **the truth and beauty ... Christ Himself** *Letters*, 12.187–77
p.83 **to persevere ... among his books** based on *Letters*, 12.187–77
p.87 **My carriage caught ... carriage for it** based on *Letters*, 11.51, 56
p.88 **To this hour I have sudden vague rushes of terror** *Letters*, 12.175
p.89 **the fire ... such devils** based on *Letters*, 4.269–70
p.93 **There never was ... of all kinds** *Letters*, 3.43
p.93 **as delicate ... I ever saw** *Letters*, 3.44
p.93–4 **I seriously believe ... cute** based on *Letters*, 3.231–32
p.94 **There is no country ... any subject** *Letters*, 3.81
p.94 **accursed and detested ... I turned back** *Letters*, 3.140, 145
p.106 **the English are ... on whom the sun shines** *Letters*, 7.294
p.106 **more amusement ... *something in motion*** *Letters*, 8.399
p.107 **in sorrow, or poverty, or ignorance** *Letters*, 5.156
p.110 **Yet nobody ever came ... to receive anybody** Forster, 13
p.110 **grow up to be a learned and distinguished man** Forster, 1.2.26
p.112 **wholly inapplicable ... now prevails** *Letters*, 3.565
p.116 **with a degree of ... in my life** "Report" 27; *Letters*, 1.106
p.117 **it was proposed to me ... quite shocking ...** *Letters*, 12.182
p.117 **a little bit of truth** *Letters*, 7.669
p.120 **"If it hadn't been for your pipe ... been nowhere"** *Letters*, 11.294
p.121 **My last special feat ... the country for breakfast** based on "Shy Neighbourhoods", 95; *Letters*, 8.489
p.122 **a whirl of dissipation ... "Beold the abazid power of woobud!"** *Letters*, 5.128
p.122 **His name was Boswell ... Boz Zwuallll!** *Letters*, 7.541

INDEX